# Become the
# MIRACLE
## the World
## is Waiting For

# Become the
# MIRACLE
## the World
## is Waiting For

---

AWAKEN YOUR GIFT, ANSWER THE CALL,
BECOME THE LIGHT

# DOUG COOPER

# Contents

# Introduction

## YOU ARE THE MIRACLE IN SOMEONE ELSE'S STORY

There is a version of you the world is waiting for.
Not a future you. Not a more polished you.
But a version already glowing inside you—an awareness,
a spark, a frequency—quietly waiting for your permission
to emerge.

This book is about remembering and becoming that.

Not by effort.
Not by fixing anything.
But by aligning with who you already are beneath the noise.

We've been taught to wait for miracles. To hope for them.
But what if your greatest transformation comes not from
receiving one—but from *becoming* one?

The truth is: you probably already have.
You've already been the miracle in someone else's story.
You just didn't know it.

That time you called someone *right when they needed it.*
That moment you said something small, but they remembered
it forever.
That hour you listened and didn't judge.
That night you stayed, or forgave, or reached across the silence.
That day you showed up, even when you were falling apart yourself.

You were the miracle.
You were the messenger.
And you didn't even realize it.

This journey is about realizing it now—and doing it on purpose.

It draws from many traditions. You'll hear echoes of Abraham-Hicks, guiding us to raise our vibration and return to the Vortex where clarity and joy reside. You'll feel the depth of Vedanta and Deepak Chopra's reminder that we are not our thoughts, not our emotions, but the awareness in which all of it moves. And you'll hear my own voice—an invitation to let your scars speak, your presence serve, and your becoming bless others in ways you may never fully see.

Because sometimes the miracle doesn't happen to you.
It happens *through* you.

And when you start living that way—aligned, awake, aware—
everything shifts.

You become the calm in someone else's chaos.
The reminder in their despair.
The light in their darkness.

Friends will feel it. Strangers will feel it.
Your family will soften.
Your presence will change rooms.

But something else happens too.
**Your life begins to feel miraculous.**
Joy rises for no reason.
Your body responds.
Your mind clears.
Your relationships deepen.
Synchronicities multiply.
You stop chasing. You start receiving.
You remember who you are—and what's always been possible.

You don't just change the world around you.
You begin to live in a new one.

This is how healing happens.
This is how lives are lifted.
One person, in alignment, becoming the miracle,
again and again and again.

You're not just here to get by.
You're here to become the one the world—and you—
have been waiting for.

**LET'S BEGIN.**

# PART I
# REFLECTIONS

---

The healing, the remembering,
the tender truths we almost missed.

# CHAPTER 1

## Learning to Love the Scar, Not Just the Healing

We talk a lot about healing.
How to move on.
How to rise above.

And it matters.

Healing can save your life.
It can save relationships, families, entire futures.

But there's something we don't talk about as much.
Something that shows up after the healing is "done."

Not loud. Not dramatic.
But persistent.

It's the scar.

It's what sticks around.
What shows up in small moments—when you thought you were past it.

It's how you know something really got to you.
Not just that you hurt,
but that you felt it all the way through.
And that it mattered.

We like to imagine healing makes us clean again.
Like if we do it well enough, no one will even know there was a wound.

But real healing leaves a trace.

Just like your body doesn't grow back smooth skin after a deep cut,
your soul doesn't either.

It patches.
It rebuilds.
But it doesn't pretend nothing happened.

Sometimes that new layer feels solid.
You forget it's there.

Other times, it pulls a little when you stretch.
Or it aches at the exact moment you thought you'd finally let go.

That doesn't mean you're broken.
It means you're alive.

It means the thing that touched you still echoes a little in your body.

Scars don't just come from tragedy or heartbreak.

They come from caring.
Trying.
Reaching.
Risking something real.

You chase a dream.
Get close to someone.
Try on a version of yourself that doesn't quite fit yet.

And then… something slips.
You miss.
You fall short.
You get burned.

And even if you heal,
you're not the same.

You don't always see the scar—but it shapes you.

Maybe it's in the way you hold back a little more now.
Or the way you try to prove you're fine when you're not.
Or the way you stop reaching altogether—just in case.

I've got a few of my own.

Here's one:
I never really learned to swim.

Technically, sure—I won't drown.
But I was never comfortable in the water.

At parties, on boats, family beach days—
I stayed on the edge.

Joked around.
Made it look like I chose not to swim.

But I didn't.

There was a fear I couldn't name,
and a wall I couldn't get past.

I built a good life anyway.
I did just fine.

But that scar?
Still shows up sometimes.

Like when I stand at the edge of something new—
and feel that same hesitation in my chest.

Here's another.
Height.

At my tallest, I was 5'8".
Now I'm less than that.

And I never thought I was short
until I stepped into certain rooms and realized who got taken seriously.

Tall men. Confident men.
Men who looked like "leaders."

Then Randy Newman came out with "Short People got no reason to live."
I know it was satire, but it didn't feel like satire in the wrong room.

I started seeing news segments on how tall men earn more.
And the data backed it up.

I didn't complain. I didn't dwell.
But something in me shrunk a little.

Not on the outside—on the inside.

I stopped expecting to lead the room.
Stopped reaching for certain things.

Didn't always notice it happening,
but I felt it.

That's what I mean by a scar.

Not all scars are big and dramatic.

Some live in the background.
They hum under the surface.

They shape your instincts before your brain has time to catch up.

They show up in who you trust.
How fast you speak.
What you let yourself want.

That boy who stayed dry at the pool?
He still shows up in me.

Not just around water.
He's there whenever I play it safe.
Whenever I laugh instead of leap.
Whenever I pretend I don't want something
because I'm not sure I'll be okay if I don't get it.

So the question isn't:
Did I ever learn to swim?

The real question is:
Can I still love the little boy who stayed dry?

The one who didn't dive in,
but stood close enough to belong.

The one who laughed at the edge,
held the towels,
watched the fun and pretended it didn't sting.

Can I bless him for trying in the only way he knew how?

Because he wasn't weak.
He was just protecting something soft.
Something sacred.

And he deserves a seat at the table—
not a shadow in the corner of my past.

That's what loving the scar means.
Not erasing it.
Not rewriting the story.

Just seeing the little one who lived through it all—
and bringing him home.

Because loving the scar isn't just seeing where you got hurt—
it's welcoming the one who felt it.

That boy?
He doesn't belong in the past.
He belongs here, now.

You don't move forward by leaving him behind.
You move forward by taking his hand—and letting him come with you.

Teddy Swims has this lyric:
"You can see my scars 'cause I'm wearin' 'em proud."

And Brené Brown says, "loving ourselves through the story
is the bravest thing we'll ever do."

Both of those hit home.

But some days, I'm not brave.
Some days I'm just tired.

Some days I'd still rather be the guy who doesn't get in the pool
than risk looking like he doesn't belong.

So I built a persona.
Long hair.
Smoked weed.
Hung out with the guys who didn't follow the rules.

I made sure no one could confuse me with the scared kid I used to be.

And it worked,
until it didn't.

Because deep down,
I was still holding that towel.
Still faking calm.
Still hoping no one would see what I was avoiding.

Maybe you've got one too.

Not about water.
But about being left behind.
Or being the loud one when quiet was expected.
Or the quiet one when everyone else was loud.

Maybe your scar taught you to disappear.
Or to perform.
Or to stay one step ahead of rejection.

And maybe you got good at it.
So good, you didn't notice you were still protecting something
that didn't need protecting anymore.

Because that's what we do.

We don't just carry scars.
We build around them.

We create personalities, patterns, careers, identities—
all to avoid the moment we never want to feel again.

But at some point,
you realize the scar's been calling the shots.

Not in a dramatic way—
just quietly steering your choices.

So what if you didn't have to keep living like that?
What if the scar doesn't mean the story's over?
What if it's just the spot where your real self started to wake up?

Loving the scar isn't about loving the pain.
It's about being honest about the path.

About who you became.
And why.
It's about sitting with the version of you who couldn't do it all,
and saying,
"You still count."

So maybe ask yourself:
What road did the scar put you on?
What habits or identities came with it?
And are they still helping you?
Or just keeping you safe?

Because the scar doesn't have to keep steering.
It can just mark the place you turned a corner.
You don't need to fix it.
You don't need to pretend it never happened.

But you do need to stop running from it.

**The scar doesn't block the miracle.**
**But hiding it might.**

And when it comes to manifesting the next chapter?

It's not about being positive all the time.
It's about being whole.

You can't fully receive what's meant for you
if you're still shoving old versions of yourself into the closet.

The moment you say:
"You get to come with me,"—
everything shifts.

That's when the miracle moves.

**Because the scar made you real.**
**Let it make you free.**

# CHAPTER 2

## The Tunnel is a Temple

What if your hardest moments weren't detours?

What if they were doorways?

**Let's talk about tunnels.**

Not the light at the end.
The tunnel itself.

The long ones.
The quiet ones.
The ones you didn't know you'd entered until something shifted—until the light behind you disappeared and the way forward wasn't clear either.

And maybe you thought:
**This can't be the way. I must've taken a wrong turn.**

But what if you didn't?
What if the tunnel wasn't a mistake…
What if it was a temple?

## WHEN THE DARKNESS FEELS LIKE DISORIENTATION
When life breaks in ways you didn't expect, the first instinct is escape.

You look for a meaning, a lesson, a loophole.

You say things like:
"This shouldn't be happening."
"I thought I already healed this."
"I must be off track."

But what if you're not off track?

What if the pain isn't a glitch...
but the very place something sacred starts to shift?

Abraham-Hicks calls it contrast—where what you don't want helps you clarify what you do.

But this isn't just contrast.
This is **conversion**.

The kind that doesn't happen in the sunshine.
It happens where the distractions fall away.
Where the light doesn't reach.
Where something inside you starts to burn clean.

## MY TUNNELS

I've walked through some.

Tunnels of leaving.
Of doubt.
Of not being chosen.
Of wondering if I still mattered when the room got quiet.

Times when the emails stopped.
When the phone stayed silent.
**Even my reflection looked like it was tired of hoping.**

Moments when I asked:
**"Is this it? Is this where I stay small?"**

But something always whispered:
**Don't decorate this place. You're not meant to live here.**
**But you are meant to pass through.**

## WHY THE TUNNEL IS SACRED

It's not a punishment.

It's a pressure chamber.

A cocoon.
A womb.
A place where who-you-were gets stripped back
until something real—something gold—starts to surface.

Not after the hard part.

**Inside it.**

That's the trick of the tunnel:
It hides the treasure in the same place it hides your hope.

And the temple?

That's not just poetry.

It's where your false gods go quiet.
Where the versions of you that used to perform or please or push through
finally stop pretending they're okay.

That's where the real voice—your soul voice—starts to speak again.

## YOU DON'T HAVE TO LOVE THE PAIN

Let's be honest: this isn't a cute little "love your struggle" message.

I'm not here to tell you to bless your wounds before you're ready.

I'm just saying—don't crawl out too early.

Don't slap a label on the lesson and move on
before the fire has finished its work.

Because you didn't come here to cope.
You came to **become**.

You came to find out what's left
when everything false starts to fall away.

## MAYBE THE TUNNEL WAS CUSTOM-MADE
For the version of you that couldn't come with you.

The identity that kept you small.
The story that kept you safe.
The performance that kept you liked—but not whole.

And once those things fall away…

you don't hear noise anymore.

You hear silence.
Then Source.
Then something deeper than both.

A presence that doesn't need polishing or defending.

It just *is*.

Trevor Hall sings,
"You can't rush your healing. Darkness has its teachings. Love is never leaving."

That one sticks.

## SO WHAT DO YOU DO IN THE TUNNEL?
Not much.

But it's not nothing.

**Don't fight the dark.**
You can light a candle. You can breathe. But don't waste your energy arguing that
it's dark. The womb is dark too.

**Talk to yourself like someone you love.**
Would you shame a friend for being in the middle of something hard? Then
don't do it to you.

**Start noticing what's still alive.**
Even in grief, there's a flicker.
Even in doubt, there's a heartbeat.
Even in loss, there's something trying to make its way toward you.

## WHAT COMES AFTER
When you come out of the tunnel—you're not the same.

You don't come out shiny.
You come out true.

You come out slower, kinder, more fluent in the language of pain.
You don't give pep talks to people in tunnels.

You sit beside them.

You say:

**"I've been here.
I know the silence.
I know the air.
And there's something beautiful just a little deeper in.
Let's stay here a while—until you feel it."**

That's the ministry born in darkness.

That's how you carry the temple with you.

## FINAL THOUGHT
If you're in a tunnel right now—

if life feels uncertain, or stripped, or still—

please don't rush yourself to the ending.

You're not broken.
You're not late.
You're not being punished.
You're being prepared.

Not for a stage.
Not for applause.
Maybe just for the sacred ordinary of becoming someone who glows in the dark.

Someone who brings light without needing to be the sun.

Someone who walks out of the tunnel with mud on their shoes and fire in their chest.

That's who we need.

Not polished saviors.
But holy messengers
who found God in the dirt
and came back glowing.

That's the real miracle.

The tunnel turned to holy ground.

# CHAPTER 3

## Not Letting Love In

*The Silent Ways We Keep Our Hearts Closed*

I want to talk about something tender.
Not just heartbreak.
Not just the people who left.
But the love we didn't let in.

Some people carry the ache of love that ended.
But others—
We carry the quieter weight
of love we never really allowed to begin.

### THE ONES I DIDN'T LET IN
Before Lorraine, there were others.

Good people. Real connections.
And if I'm honest—I didn't let them in.

I talked myself out of it. Told myself it was too much.
Too soft. Too safe.
Too different from what I thought love was supposed to feel like.

Some of them showed up with open hearts.
And I pulled back—because I didn't recognize that kind of love yet.

It didn't match the old pattern.
It didn't come with the same tension I'd confused for chemistry.

I don't carry guilt about it.
But I do carry the truth.

That I missed some beautiful things
because I wasn't ready to believe I deserved them.

## THEN CAME LORRAINE
She saw me before I knew how to see myself.
She didn't try to fix me.
Didn't push. She just… stayed.

**And slowly, I started to feel safe in a way I hadn't before.**

She didn't feel like a test.
She felt like a remembering.

And little by little, I began to let love in—
not just hers, but my own.

## THE SILLY, HUMAN REASONS
Of course, not every missed love comes from a deep psychological wound.
Sometimes, we bail for reasons so dumb we don't even say them out loud.

So here's to the Great Almosts:
The people we might've said yes to—if not for one little thing.

"He brought soup on a picnic."
"She didn't like Mexican food."
"She had a crystal named Brad."
"He said 'supposably.'"
"Her laugh was… cartoonish."
"She wasn't a bad kisser—just not a great one."
"My friends said I could do better. So I believed them."

We say we're looking for love.
But sometimes?

We're just looking for an exit.

## THE REAL REASONS WE CLOSE THE DOOR

Underneath the funny stories,
there's usually something heavier.

Sometimes we don't let love in
not because of their soup or their shoes—but because something in us
got trained to flinch when love gets too close.

If we could pull back the curtain,
we'd probably find a few stories
playing on repeat in a lot of hearts.

**We're afraid of being seen.**

We want to be loved—but only for the version of us we've polished up.
The one that's witty and put together
and never too needy.

But when someone really sees us—the soft spots, the shame,
the stuff we've hidden—we panic.

So we leave first.

**We're still grieving.**

Not always loudly.
Sometimes in ways even we don't notice.

An old love.
A breakup we "got over" but never really felt.
The person we used to be before things changed.

We think we're ready—but part of us is still sitting beside a loss
that hasn't been named yet.

**We've mistaken peace for boredom.**

We've known chaotic love.
Unpredictable love.
Love that kept us guessing.
So when someone shows up
calm and grounded and actually available—we think something's off.

Not enough spark.
Too easy.
Must not be real.

So we ghost the one who might've been the safest thing we'd ever known.

**We believed someone who told us we weren't lovable.**

Maybe it was a parent.
Maybe it was an ex.
Maybe it was just one moment
that landed wrong and stayed too long.

Even now—years later—that voice still runs the script.

So when love shows up, we assume it's a mistake.

Or a trick.
Or temporary.

And we prepare for it to end
before it even begins.

**We gave up quietly.**

We still smile.
Still swipe.
Still play the part.

But somewhere inside—we stopped believing love was coming.
And instead of telling someone, we buried it.
Even from ourselves.

## A GENTLE TRUTH

If any of that sounds like you—it's okay.

You're not broken.
You're not too late.
You're not behind.

You just learned how to protect your heart
before you learned how to trust it.

And honestly?
That was smart.

You did what you had to do to stay safe in a world that didn't always feel safe.

So maybe now, it's not about blaming yourself
for what you couldn't open to back then.

Maybe it's about learning to open now—in a way that feels kind, not forced.

## COMING BACK TO OPENNESS

The good news?

Love doesn't disappear.
It doesn't get mad.
It doesn't keep score.

It just waits.

You don't have to chase it.
You don't need to fix your profile
or rewrite your story
or fly to a retreat in the jungle.

You just have to notice
when something kind shows up
and your first instinct is to push it away.

That's the moment.

That's the doorway.

You pause.
You breathe.
You ask yourself,
**"Is this really about them—or about an old habit in me?"**

And maybe,
instead of running,
you stay.

Not forever.
Not with urgency.
Just long enough
to sit beside the part that's still flinching—
and let it feel,
maybe for the first time,
that it doesn't have to anymore.

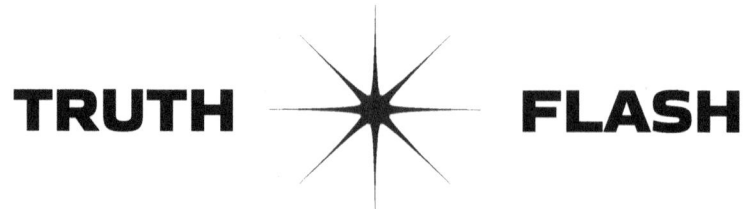

# TRUTH ✦ FLASH

## *Let Them Love You Out Loud*

When I told my friend Lee about my first speaking event,
he didn't even pause.

"I'll take care of the little cocktail tables," he said.
"I'll make some flower arrangements. Just let me do it."

And what did I say?

The thing we've all been taught to say:
**"Oh no, you don't have to do that."**

But then I caught myself.

Because I remembered something Abraham once said:
**You can't be a match to abundance and block it at the same time.**

And I thought of what Deepak teaches—
that giving and receiving are part of the same field,
always moving,
always connected.

So I tried something different.
I looked at Lee, and I said:
**"Thank you. That would mean a lot."**

It felt simple.
But it wasn't easy.

Because sometimes,
the work isn't being more generous.

It's being more *receivable*.

Sometimes the spiritual growth isn't in what you give—
it's in what you let yourself accept.

**Not because you owe.**
**Not because you earned it.**
**But because the Universe is trying to reach you**
**through someone who's already standing there with open hands.**

And if you deflect it,
you don't just block the gift—
you block the blessing.
For both of you.

So next time someone reaches out with love,
or kindness,
or beauty—

Don't shrink.
Don't explain.
Don't wave it away.

Let it land.
Let it soften something in you.
Let it stay.

**Let them love you out loud.**

# CHAPTER 4

## It Rhymes,
## But It's Not the Same Song

You've probably felt it—
that quiet resistance that rises
right when something new starts to open.

It could be a relationship.
A job lead.
A creative idea.
A part of you that finally wants more.

And then—
tension.

Your chest tightens.
Your shoulders brace.
And a voice inside whispers:
**"I know this one.**
**I've heard how this ends."**

So you back off.
You say, "I'm not ready."
Or, "I've tried this before."
Or, "This isn't me."

But maybe that's not the truth.
Maybe that's just the rhythm of something old
echoing inside something new.

Yes, it rhymes.
But it's not the same song.

## THE PATTERN

This doesn't just happen in love.

It shows up when someone wants to speak up—
but remembers the last time they got shut down.

When someone wants to create again—
but recalls the silence that came after sharing something vulnerable.

When someone wants to care for their body—
but remembers the times they started and didn't stick with it,
so now the idea of trying again feels like a setup.

When someone has a hunger, a calling, a pull—
but all they can hear is the faint echo of last time.
The crash. The letdown. The silence after the dream.

The words may be different.
The timing might be better.
But the emotional memory is loud.

And so we confuse the feeling of familiarity
with the certainty of failure.

But that's not wisdom.
That's a wound—
looping.

## THE TRUTH

Yes, life has patterns.
But not every pattern is a prophecy.

Just because something *feels* familiar
doesn't mean it's headed for the same ending.

Here's the thing most people miss:

**You are not the same.**
You've grown.
You've healed.
You've learned things the hard way.
You're walking in with better instincts, better boundaries, better questions.
So maybe the question isn't:
**"Is this safe?"**
Maybe it's:
**"Am I willing to let this be different—because I am?"**

## FIVE REFLECTIONS WHEN OLD FEAR MEETS NEW OPPORTUNITY

If something good starts to show up—
and fear follows, not because it's wrong,
but because it *feels* like something you've been through—
pause here:

**1. What part of me is reacting?**
Is this my grounded self?
Or is this the version of me who got shut down, left out, or burned?

**2. What's actually different this time?**
New people.
New timing.
New you.

**3. What have I learned since then?**
You may have failed before.
But now you have better tools.
That matters.

**4. What pace feels wise?**
You don't have to leap.
You can go slow.
You can stay present, one step at a time.

**5. Am I showing up new—or still playing the old role?**
Sometimes what repeats isn't the situation.
It's us.
We show up with the same fears, same walls, same story—
and then say, "See? It always ends like this."

But if you show up differently,
the moment has a chance to be different too.

## THE INVITATION
So maybe it's not about whether life is repeating itself.
Maybe it's about whether we are.

You don't have to be fearless.
You don't have to be perfect.

You just have to be honest
about what energy you're bringing into the room.

This moment might *look* like the past—
but that doesn't mean it's carrying the same truth.

So if something in your life feels like it's circling back,
don't run just because the rhythm feels familiar.

Pause. Breathe.
Ask better questions.
Stay one moment longer than you did last time.

Yes—it may rhyme.
But this isn't the same song.

Not unless you stop it
before the next verse begins.

You still have something to say.
You still hold the pen.
And the ending?

The last line is still yours to write.

# CHAPTER 5

## The Sacred Cows in the Room

*What we protect instead of heal.*
*What we avoid instead of feel.*

I had a moment recently where I realized—
I've been protecting something
that might not be protecting me.

It's not a big thing.
Or maybe it is.

It's weed.

I still smoke, even though it hurts my throat.
Even though I say I want clarity, connection, momentum—
and I know it dulls all three.
But it's there, like this untouchable part of my day.

And that's when it hit me:
This is one of my sacred cows.

Without it, I feel less creative.
Less inspired.
My head is clearer when I don't smoke,
but there's this fear I'll miss a great idea,

or a revelation,
or some version of magic I've trained myself to expect.

I've been smoking, in some form, for almost 60 years.
It's not good for my health. I know that.
My wife rolls her eyes every time I mention it.
So I sneak around,
like a teenager,
even though half the time she sniffs me out anyway.

## WHAT SACRED COWS LOOK LIKE

Sacred cows are like that.
They're the things we've outgrown,
but still protect.

Some are physical—
an old habit, the clothes we always wear,
the topics we never touch but always feel nearby.

Some are emotional—
beliefs about how relationships are supposed to work.

How emotions are supposed to be handled.
How people are supposed to change (or not).

Some are spiritual—
rules we made decades ago,
still quietly calling the shots behind the scenes.

Some live inside our families—
the things no one is allowed to mention.
The subjects that carry so much charge
we've all silently agreed to pretend they don't exist.

Some are ancestral.
Ways we were taught to act.
To stay silent.
To forgive too quickly.
To stay one step ahead of disapproval.

## WHERE THE PHRASE COMES FROM

The phrase sacred cow comes from Hindu tradition,
where cows are honored—symbols of life, nourishment, nonviolence.
They're not to be harmed.
They're allowed to lie down in the road.
You don't move them.
You just work around them.

Western culture picked up the phrase—
not as reverence, but as a warning:
Here's the thing you're not allowed to question.

In business, it's the outdated system no one will update.
In families, it's the person no one confronts.
In identity, it's the survival story we're afraid to stop telling.

But sacred cows don't stay sacred.
They solidify.
They block roads.
They keep us from saying what we need to say.

## WHEN THE SACRED COW IS THE GLUE

In a lot of relationships,
the sacred cow becomes the glue.

It's the thing you both agreed on early—
maybe without ever saying it out loud.

A rule.
A rhythm.
Something that helped you feel steady
when life wasn't.

And maybe it worked for a while.

It made things feel safe. Predictable.
It kept the peace.
It helped you get through seasons
you weren't sure you'd survive.

But over time,
the rule starts running the relationship.
And no one questions it—
because to question it feels like
pulling at the thread that holds everything together.

So when one person starts to grow—
starts to want more truth,
or space,
or softness,
or something new—

and the other person is still clinging to the old pattern—

it doesn't just feel like change.
It feels like betrayal.

Not because it is.
But because the thing you were both leaning on
is suddenly moving.
And that's terrifying.

## THE SHARED SACRED COWS WE DON'T TALK ABOUT

Some sacred cows are quiet agreements between two people—
the kind that form slowly over time,
until one day they're just how things are.

"We do everything together."
At first, it feels like closeness.
Over time, it becomes a rule.
And when one person needs space, the other feels abandoned.

"Don't bring up money."
Maybe it caused fights in the past.
Now it's off-limits—so nothing grows, nothing heals, and resentment
starts to fill the silence.

"I'm the fixer, you're the one who struggles."
One person always rescues,
the other always falls apart.
It becomes their identity—until one of them starts to shift,
and the roles don't work anymore.

"We don't fight."
Sounds healthy, but usually means:
We don't tell the truth when it might cause discomfort.
Conflict doesn't disappear—it just hides in other places.

"Your success is my threat."
No one says it, but one person starts growing—
and the other pulls back, subtly,
afraid the relationship won't survive the expansion.

These aren't bad people.
These are just old rules.
They helped things work.
Until one person starts to grow—and the rule can't keep up.

## WHAT'S YOURS?
Maybe something's already raising its hand.
You've outgrown it, but you're still protecting it.

A habit.
A role.
A belief about who you have to be to stay loved.

Don't judge it.
Just notice it.

Then ask:
Is it helping me breathe?
Or is it making me smaller?

Not everything we hold sacred
was meant to last forever.

Some things are sacred
because they once saved us.

And it's okay
to thank them—
and still decide to let them go.

## SO WHAT DO YOU DO WITH A SACRED COW?
Not every sacred cow needs to be thrown out. Some of them are still useful—
but only if we're honest about what they are.

You might name it.
Acknowledge it.
Say out loud, "This helped me once. Maybe it still does."

And if it doesn't— maybe it's time to let it go.

Not in anger.
Not with shame.
But with clarity.

Because you're not the same person who built that rule.
And your life might need different scaffolding now.

The ones worth keeping will feel like support.
The ones that are finished will feel like a weight.
One will make you exhale.
The other will make you brace.

One will sound like truth.
The other will sound like a version of you
trying not to get hurt again.

## THE INVITATION
So take a look.
In your work.
Your relationships.
Your identity.

Are you holding something sacred
just because you're afraid
to see who you'd be without it?

Sometimes the most spiritual thing you can do
is ask the question you were told not to ask.

Sometimes the most loving thing you can do
is stretch the story
until the truth can breathe again.

And sometimes the most powerful thing you can do—
is bless the cow…
and move on.

# CHAPTER 6

## The Grief of Almost

*The ache of what could've been. The healing of what still can.*

There's a kind of grief we don't talk about much. Not the grief of death. Not the grief of disaster.

But the grief of *almost*.

The job we nearly landed. The person we nearly loved. The version of ourselves we almost became.

There's no funeral for those losses. No ceremony. No cards in the mail. Just a silence where a story might've lived.

Sometimes we feel it as a dull ache. Sometimes it knocks the wind out of us in the middle of an ordinary afternoon.

And sometimes— we don't even know that's what we're carrying. We just feel... behind. Or off. Or like something slipped through our fingers when we weren't looking.

We try to shrug it off. We say it wasn't meant to be. We tell ourselves we're over it.

But some part of us still stands there, holding the shape of the thing that never quite arrived.

We build stories around it: "It wouldn't have worked." "They didn't really love me." "I probably couldn't have handled it."

But grief doesn't care about logic. It just wants to be felt.
And the grief of almost— it's real.

It can shape how we see ourselves. How we trust. How wide a window we leave open for joy to find us again.

Sometimes we hold back now because the last time we went all in, life didn't meet us there.

So we dim the dream. Shrink the desire. Tell ourselves we're fine with less. But we're not here to make peace with almost. We're here to become whole again.

Not by pretending the past didn't matter. Not by erasing the ache. But by making room for the truth:

**Something hurt us.** And we're still worthy of joy.

**Something was lost.** And we still get to go forward.

We don't have to stay in waiting rooms for doors that already closed. We can grieve what we needed to grieve— and then walk back into the light.

There are still new versions of us that haven't even gotten their chance yet. Still ideas waiting to be born. Still rooms we haven't lit up. Still love that hasn't heard our name.

Let's not close the book on ourselves too soon.

Let's grieve what we almost were— and then become who we're still here to be. Let's turn the ache, the almost, and the pause— into a deeper, wiser yes.

Because maybe the door wasn't closing. Maybe it was clearing space for something truer to come through.

We haven't missed our moment. We're still the ones who get to say yes—to the next dream, the next try, the next miracle waiting to meet us when we show up whole.

## EVERY PROFESSION HAS ITS ALMOSTS

The surgeon who almost chose to work in the refugee camps.
The chef who nearly opened her own restaurant before the economy turned.
The dancer who got the callback but didn't make the second cut—and never auditioned again.

Even success doesn't protect us from this grief.
Ask the lawyer who always wondered what it would have been like to write novels.
Or the CEO who wanted to teach first grade.
Or the retiree who wonders what would've happened if she had taken that chance to move to Paris.

This is not about failure. It's about threshold.
The moments where we almost walked through the door. And didn't.

**And maybe what we almost became... still left us something.**
A spark.
A hunger.
A tenderness toward others who almost made it too.

What we grieve, we also grow from.
What we missed, we still carry as knowing.
And what we couldn't reach back then—
might just become the compass for what we choose now.

Because we don't come out of the grief of almost empty-handed.
We come out wiser.
Softer.
More ready.

The next part of us isn't a stranger.
It's the one who walked through that ache
and kept going.

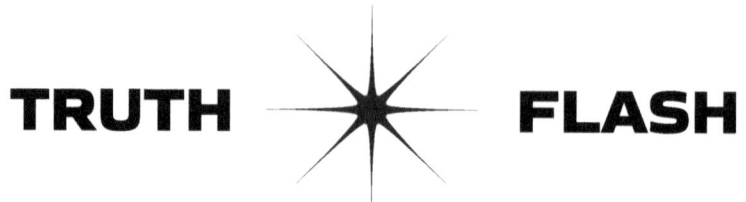

# TRUTH ✦ FLASH

## *ENVY: The Whisper of a Life Still Calling*

We don't envy what we don't recognize.

You don't envy the woman dancing barefoot under the stars unless some part of you once longed to feel that free—before you got careful, before you decided it was safer to be quiet than to be seen.

You don't envy the man who walks into a room like he belongs unless something in you still aches to feel that worthy.

Envy doesn't come from nowhere.
It doesn't mean they have too much.
It means we've buried a wanting that never really left.

It's a bruise over a hidden longing.
A vibration that says: "You once wanted this. You still do. But you've talked yourself out of it."

### CHARLIE, MOSES, AND THE TENTH COMMANDMENT

The famous investor Charlie Munger once said,
"It's not greed that drives the world. It's envy."

And he would know.

This is a man who studied markets and behavior for nearly a century.
He didn't point to war or poverty or trauma. He pointed to envy—
the quiet destroyer. The one we're embarrassed to admit.

He even brought up the Tenth Commandment—
the one most people forget.

"Thou shalt not covet thy neighbor's wife... nor his house... nor anything that is
thy neighbor's."

Why would that one matter so much?
Because it pulls us away from our own life.
From our own joy.
From our own becoming.

Envy doesn't just hurt others.
It starves us.
It distracts us.
It keeps us staring at someone else's light while ignoring our own spark.

## INVERTING THE ENVY
Charlie also taught something called inversion:
"If you want to avoid misery, figure out what causes it—and don't do that."

So let's invert envy.

Ask yourself:
What would make envy impossible?
What belief would make comparison irrelevant?

Maybe this:
Envy disappears not when others lose what they have...
But when you reclaim what you left behind.

It disappears when you stop pretending.

When you say:
"I want that, too. And maybe I still can."

## TRY THIS SIMPLE INVERSION EXERCISE
The next time envy shows up—don't push it away.
Flip it.
Let it name what you thought was gone.
Let it point you back to something you buried
before it had a chance to live.

Envy is a spotlight.
Use it to illuminate the path back to your own becoming.

## FINAL REFLECTION

Envy isn't about them.
It's about you—
the version of you still waiting to be chosen.
By you.

It's not a flaw.
It's not a sin.
It's not a shame spiral.
It's a signal.

And the moment you listen—
not to punish yourself,
but to turn toward what still wants to live in you—
that's when envy becomes a gift.

**Envy is a signpost.**
**Not to what they have—but to what you still want.**
**Let it guide you home.**

# PART II
# EXPANSIONS

The becoming, the light, the aligned action—
and the joy of showing up true.

# Not Everyone Gets a Seat in Your Dressing Room"

*A message about creativity, courage, and claiming your sacred space*

There comes a moment—maybe more than one—when we step into something new. We try something different. We share something honest. We post something we actually care about. And suddenly, we're not just living our regular lives anymore—We're onstage!

We've stretched ourselves. We've shown something. We've made ourselves visible. And then it happens.

Someone we thought would clap… doesn't. Someone else makes a weird comment. Someone we haven't heard from in years suddenly wants to "offer advice." And we're left wondering: "Wait… did I do something wrong?"

Here's the truth we've come to: **Not everyone gets a seat in your dressing room.**

The dressing room is sacred. It's not for critics. It's not for people who aren't willing to risk their own becoming. It's where we stretch. Where we change. Where we get ready to walk out as more of who we really are. We don't let just anybody in there.

Think for a moment: Who have we let into our dressing room that didn't belong. Whose silence still echoes in our heads? Who did we imagine would be proud of us—and instead, they just… weren't? We're not alone in that.

## FIVE REASONS PEOPLE DON'T CLAP

Let's offer a little grace here, because sometimes people don't clap— and it's not really about us.

Some people don't know how to support what they don't understand. They're not mean. They're just uncomfortable. They miss the old us. The one who didn't paint. Or speak. Or say what we really think. Our growth unsettles the roles they still live inside.

Some people are jealous—but they'd never admit it. Our courage makes them feel their own stillness. And that's not our fault—but they may distance themselves.

Some unconsciously want us to fail. It's not cruelty—it's fear. If we can change, then they could have too. And that truth is unbearable if they've never tried.

Some are just plain threatened. Especially if our creativity defies their "rules." They want us to stay in our lane. But our soul never agreed to lanes.

Some people are grieving their own unlived life. Our becoming brings up their silence. And instead of cheering, they go quiet—or awkward—or absent.

And sometimes… they just don't like what we made. What we did, didn't move them. It didn't speak to them. And that's okay too. It may not mean anything more than that. Their response doesn't have to define our direction.

But listen closely: That's not a reflection of our worth. It's a reflection of their wiring. And their wiring doesn't get to reprogram our truth.

If we're stretching right now— Trying something new, saying something real, creating something honest, changing our rhythm, or finally showing up as more of ourselves— We get to choose who gets a seat in that sacred space.

And if someone's presence makes us question our voice, second-guess our power, or apologize for our truth— then we can thank them for their concern, and ask them to wait outside.

We like to think it's other people who doubt us, who hold us back, who question our readiness. But the real critic? The one with the harshest voice, the coldest glare, and the most unreasonable expectations—is usually already in the room. It's us.

We second-guess our talent. We shrink our shine to make others comfortable. We rehearse the worst-case scenario instead of stepping into our light. And as Marianne Williamson reminds us:

"Our deepest fear is that we are powerful beyond measure.
It is our light, not our darkness, that most frightens us."
—Marianne Williamson, *A Return to Love*

Because if we truly let ourselves be seen—fully, brilliantly, unapologetically—it would change everything. And that kind of power? It's terrifying…
until it's not.

And Michelle Obama said:
"If you don't get out there and define yourself, you'll be quickly and inaccurately defined by others."

Because if we don't speak our truth, someone else will speak it for us—and they'll get it wrong.

Our dressing room is where the real us gets ready. It's where the nervousness meets the calling. It's where our past selves watch us apply our present courage. And it's where our future self nods and says, "Yes. This is who we came to be."

So let's remember this: We don't need everyone to clap. We just need to show up, walk out, and deliver the one thing only we can offer.

The real us. The becoming us. The one who knows—

**Not everyone gets a seat in your dressing room.**
But you? You get to take center stage.

# PART II: CHAPTER 2

# Parallel Lives:
# The Ones I Could Still Be

I used to think parallel lives were science fiction— some strange Star Trek concept where an alternate version of you makes different choices and ends up in a different life.

But now I wonder if it's much simpler than that.

Maybe parallel lives are the ones we can still live. The version of us who moves to Italy. The one who has a baby late in life. The one who starts painting again. The one who leaves the safe job. The one who dares to love.

Not because we have to do all of them—but because just knowing they exist changes us.

We tend to mourn the lives we didn't live. We say "I missed my chance" or "It's too late" or "That version of me is gone." But what if that version of us is still very much alive? Waiting. Still available—not in the past, but in our field. In our Vortex. In the creative matrix of who we are becoming.

We can wake up tomorrow and say, "I think I'm ready to try being that one now."

And yes, maybe some versions are no longer practical. Maybe the body doesn't bend like it once did. Maybe that door did close. But the essence of it—what we wanted to feel in that life—is still available to us.

There are lives we haven't lived yet. Versions of us that never left—just waited. Not behind us, but beside us. Still ready. Still possible.

If the goal was to feel bold, or adventurous, or wild, or adored… we can still have that.

There are versions of us who know how. Versions who were never ashamed. Versions who made different choices and didn't get stuck in the story.

They're not gone. They're just waiting for us to remember.

So next time you feel envy rise up—or longing—or curiosity— Pause and ask: What version of me just knocked on the door? Which one of me still wants to be lived? What would it take to give them a chance?

We don't have to quit our jobs, sell our house, and start over. We just have to let them in a little. One small decision that belongs to that version of us. One conversation they would say yes to. One piece of clothing they would wear. One hour spent like that other life was already ours.

Call it quantum living. Call it remembering. Call it grace.

But don't call it too late. Because it's not. Not for the ones we could still be.

## WHAT ABRAHAM-HICKS SAYS ABOUT IT

Abraham doesn't always use the term "parallel lives" the way science fiction does. But they absolutely teach that multiple versions of us already exist in vibrational form.

The joyful one. The healed one. The successful, free, fulfilled one.

Not theoretical versions—real ones. Already formed. Already ready.

We don't have to build them. We just have to tune to them.

If we think a thought that matches that version's reality—and feel the feeling of already being there—we're no longer wishing for it. We're living into it.

That version of us becomes our current frequency. And the longer we hold that signal, the more our real life begins to reflect it.

## WHAT DEEPAK CHOPRA ADDS

Deepak calls it the field of all possibilities. Every potential version of us exists there. Not bound by time. Not limited by identity.

We connect to that field through awareness. Stillness. Presence.

He calls this our nonlocal self—the self beyond biography or personality or memory. The self that already is everything we could become.

When we rest in that self, we don't need to imagine our potential. We feel it. We become it. We choose it.

And then, what seemed like an alternate life becomes the one we're actually living.

## THE REAL MIRACLE

Whether we call it vibration or consciousness, attraction or awareness, the message is the same:

We are not limited to the life we've been living. There are other versions of us— not just imaginary, but real, vibrant, ready to be remembered.

So next time we feel the nudge—that flicker of "What if I...?"—don't dismiss it. That might not be fantasy. That might be our other life reaching for us.

And us? We might just be ready to reach back.

# PART II: CHAPTER 3

# The Empty Cup is as Sweet as the Punch

*Letting Go, Not Because You Failed—But Because You Finished*

*"The empty cup is as sweet as the punch."*
—from the song *Along Comes Mary* by The Association, 1966

I'm not sure what they meant when they wrote it, but I heard that line one morning—somewhere between sleep and waking—and it made me laugh out loud.

I'd been lying there, waiting for inspiration for this book. That's how a lot of my chapter titles arrive—sneaky little truths that drift in before the world fully wakes up.

And then, this one:
"The empty cup is as sweet as the punch."

It cracked something open.

Because honestly? The empty cup is sweet. It's open. It's clear. It's ready. It can hold the next big idea, the next revelation, the next creative storm. It doesn't have to cling to what it used to hold. And in that way, it might even be better than full.

The cup isn't empty because it failed.
It's empty because it's ready.

## CAROLE AND THE COURAGE TO POUR IT ALL OUT

My friend Carole is a creative force. She walked the El Camino pilgrimage, and from that experience—and many others in her bold, rich life—she wrote and professionally recorded a full album of original songs.

She shared it. Promoted it. Honored it. She did the whole thing, all in.

And then—without fanfare—she emptied the cup.

She moved on to painting. Now she's making layered, soulful visual art that speaks its own language. And when that's done? She'll probably empty that cup too.

Not because it didn't matter—
but because it did.
And it's complete.

## THE SACRED SPACE OF EMPTINESS

In Buddhism, emptiness is not about absence.
It's about non-attachment. Openness.
About releasing identity, ego, and clinging to form so we can
receive reality as it truly is.

Buddha once said that the usefulness of a cup comes from its emptiness.
Its shape matters—but only because it makes space.

Even in Scripture, we find echoes of this: Psalm 23 says, "My cup runneth over."
But for it to overflow, it had to be emptied first.

So maybe emptiness isn't lack.
Maybe it's the holiest form of preparation.

## ABRAHAM'S GRID AND THE SPACE BETWEEN

Abraham teaches that when we stop trying to force outcomes,
and instead build a Grid of general well-being—
"I like this moment."
"I like feeling ease."
"I like who I'm becoming"—we become receptive.

Trying to pour more into a cup that's already full blocks the flow.
But an empty cup?
That's where new things land.

## HOW TO LIVE THE EMPTY CUP

Finish the thing. Then bless it and release it.
Don't confuse effort with value. Rest is a form of readiness.
Let emptiness be fertile. Not hollow—holy.
Become the vessel, not the contents. You are not what you produce.
Say: "That was beautiful. I'm ready for what's next."

You don't have to pour to prove.
You don't have to stay full to matter.

Sometimes, the sweetest thing is the space
where something new can enter.

And maybe that's the gift: the space itself—the echo of something
beautiful that already poured through you, and the hush that says you're
ready for what's next.

# PART II: CHAPTER 4

# The Season Was Enough

## THE BIRDS KNOW THE WAY

Every spring, we get visitors to our house. Not people—but birds.
Little ones. Yellow-colored. Red-breasted. Quick, joyful, and full of purpose.

They build nests above our balcony.
They drink from our little fountain out back.
And they love the sticky nectar in the bird of paradise flowers that pop open
just once a year, ready for their arrival.

And then—just as magically as they came—they're gone.

The flowers dry up.
The nests are left empty.
The air goes quiet.

## THE BEAUTY OF A BRIEF SEASON

I've come to see something beautiful in the rhythm of our birds.
These birds show up.
They build, they sing, they eat, they raise a little family...
And then they move on.

They don't cling to the balcony.
They don't mourn the flower when it withers.
They don't second-guess their instincts.
They trust the cycle.
They come when it's time.

And they leave when it's time.
And not once do they question if it was worth it.

That, to me, feels like wisdom.

## THE MYSTERY OF SHOWING UP

I've been married three times.

The first—my college sweetheart—makes sense in the way that young love often does.
We were in the same chapter of life, and there's not much mystery in how that happened.

The third—well, she's still with me. And I'm grateful every day.

But the second?

That one remains a mystery.
We didn't have much in common, except maybe for football, baseball, and recreational drugs.
And it didn't end well.
No one I knew thought it would last—and they weren't wrong.

I used to ask myself: What was that all about?
But over time, I've stopped needing an answer.
Because not every season comes with an explanation.
Some things... just arrive, leave their lessons and marks, and disappear as quickly as they came.

Like those birds.
They build their nests, make a little noise, maybe even leave a mess—
And then they're gone.
This year, they left a dead baby bird on the balcony railing the day they left.
I feel like they wanted to thank us for being their partners in this year's migration.
And tell us that everyone survived, but would we please give this baby a proper burial?

We could take the nests down every year.
Keep the balcony clean.

Make sure they don't come back.

But we've chosen to let them do their thing.
To let them show up and do what they came to do—whatever that is.

Maybe that second marriage was like that.
A visit. A chapter. A season.
A chance for us both to evolve, even if we didn't see it at the time.

## LETTING IT BE ENOUGH

That's the part I keep coming back to:

What if some things are meant to be brief?
What if some chapters aren't supposed to last—but they were supposed to happen?

Of course, the nest was meant to be built… even if it didn't stay.
What if the love was real… even if it didn't last?

## THE WISDOM OF THE BIRDS

The birds don't need a reason.
They don't apologize when they leave.
They don't try to force a longer stay.
They just… trust.
They trust the nectar will be there again next year.
They trust the instinct that says, go now.
And they trust the return—if and when it comes.

There's a spiritual practice in that.
In letting something be enough because it happened.
Not because it lasted.
Not because it was easy.
Not because it fit some ideal.

But because it was the time of the season.

## A BLESSING FOR THE NEST AND THE LEAVING

Some of us are still trying to make sense of a past relationship.
A career that started and ended quickly.
A dream that bloomed for one season and faded.
Something that came and went—and left us wondering, *What was that all for?*

Maybe the answer is: You showed up.
It was just that season's turn.
You were the bird. Or the flower. Or the one who watched it all in awe.

And maybe—that's enough.

Let the mystery be part of the beauty.
Let the mess be part of the offering.
Let the briefness be part of the blessing.

And when something arrives in your life—
A person.
A moment.
An opportunity.
A call to love…

Let it build its nest.

Let it be what it came to be.

And when it's time to let it go—
Do that with just as much reverence.

Because in the great rhythm of it all—
Sometimes the season is enough.

# PART II: CHAPTER 5

# What Does the World Need From Us Now

*(And How I Almost Didn't Answer the Call)*

## THE QUESTION THAT FOUND ME

This chapter is called "What Does the World Need From Me Now?"
But the truth is—I didn't come up with that title because I had the answer.
I came up with it because it haunted me.

I started hearing it in the quiet moments. On walks. In dreams. In the ache of another good idea I left behind. And at first, I thought it was a question about purpose or career or projects. But eventually, I realized:
It was a quiet invitation—one I kept hearing but kept setting aside.

And for a while, I didn't answer it.

## THE ALMOSTS AND THE CONTRASTS

I've had big ideas before. Good ones. Maybe even great ones.
Books that felt divinely inspired. Workshops that mapped themselves out in the margins of my journals. A hundred or a thousand business ideas that were foolproof. Talks I could already feel people responding to—before I ever said a word.

And yet... I walked away. Closed the laptop. Put the plan in a drawer with all the others.

Maybe you've done that too?

There's a quiet ache in the space where something wanted to be born—and wasn't. A low hum of sadness for the version of us that didn't step forward.

And I want to be honest about what stops me.
It's not logistics. It's not time. It's not money.
It's that voice.

You know the one.

"Who's going to care?"
"People won't show up if I speak."
"They won't buy the book if I write it."
"They'll think I'm full of myself. Or worse, they just won't think about me at all."

That voice doesn't yell. It whispers. Right at the moment I'm about to move forward.
And it sounds so reasonable, so self-protective, that sometimes I believe it.

Every single time I've stopped myself in the past, that was the voice that convinced me.

But here's what I've realized:
That voice isn't my wisdom. It's not my intuition. It's just fear I hadn't faced yet—disguised to sound like humility or wisdom.

And the real tragedy isn't that the world missed out. It's that I missed out—on the joy of completing what was mine to give.

**THE VERSION OF ME WHO FINISHES**
There was a time I thought I had a procrastination problem.
That I just needed more discipline, more structure, more...whatever.

But what I've come to understand is this:

Failure or not following through isn't something to get mad at yourself about. It's not a moral issue. It's not proof of anything. Most of the time, it's just misalignment—nothing more, nothing less.

I just wasn't aligned with the version of me who finishes.

But He existed.

The Vortex—according to Abraham-Hicks—is the energetic place where everything you've ever truly wanted already exists in vibrational form. Every desire you've ever had, every loving version of you, every fulfilled outcome—it's already there, waiting for you to become a match to it.

So when I say, "He (I) was in the Vortex," I mean... He (I) was ready.
But I wasn't a match yet.

So I started using a tool called The Grid—also from Abraham-Hicks. The Grid is how you build the emotional scaffolding to receive what's in the Vortex.
It's not about checking boxes or setting goals. It's about choosing the feelings that match what you want—and letting those feelings come first.

You fill in the Grid by asking, "How do I want to feel?" And then you feel it.
You sit in it. You practice it.

From that emotional state—calm, clear, connected—your actions start to line up effortlessly.

I stopped trying to force action from a place of pressure. And I started asking:
"What does the version of me who finishes feel like?"

And here's what came up:
Calm
Clear
Capable
Energized
On purpose
Joyfully pulled—not painfully pushed

And day by day... I started stepping into him. Not all at once. Not perfectly.
But enough.

Enough to stand here now and say:
"I'm finishing this one. This big project. This message. This calling—
because it's not just a task. It's a trust."

## WHAT GETS IN THE WAY

Before we go further, let's revisit the idea of alignment.

Alignment is that deep, steady feeling that your thoughts, energy, and emotions are flowing together—where you feel in sync with yourself and maybe even something greater. It's not a rigid state of perfection. It's more like resonance. Harmony.

And one thing I've learned is this:

Negative emotion doesn't help you get there. In fact, it sets you back and slows down positive momentum.

Sometimes we act like negative emotion is useful—like guilt will motivate us, or shame will teach us, or self-criticism will keep us honest.

But the truth is, it just doesn't lead in any positive direction.

Negative emotion isn't the path to alignment. It's the sign that we're on a path that's out of step with our truth.

Your Inner Being—your highest self—doesn't speak in shame. It speaks in clarity, in encouragement, in peace.

So if I'm feeling bad, it's not a cosmic punishment. It's a cue. It's just my guidance system saying, "You've started telling a story that isn't true."

Stories like:
"I'm too late."
"I should've done more by now."
"No one wants what I have to offer."

And my Inner Being quietly says:
"That's not my story. Come back to the one that is."

## WHAT I'M BEGINNING TO TRUST

So what came next?

Not a polished plan. Not a fully formed offering. Just a quiet sense that maybe…
maybe I could begin again.

Not for attention. Not for applause. Just because something in me felt ready to
say yes.

I started to write again. To speak again. To listen to the pull, not the pressure.

And as I did, I felt that earlier question—"What does the world need from me
now?"—shift from a haunting into a kind of homecoming.

I don't have all the answers yet. I'm still stepping into this version of myself. But
I know this much:

**Saying yes to what feels true—before it's fully formed—is its own kind of
miracle.**

And for me, with my big project, that yes is starting right here, with this
moment, with you.

## WHAT THE WORLD MIGHT NEED FROM US

So I'll leave you with the same question I asked of myself, that started it all:

What does the world need from you now?

Not five years ago. Not someday. Not when you're retired. Not when you find a
girlfriend or boyfriend or a soulmate. Not when you've healed more, learned
more, lost more weight, made more money, or figured it all out.

Now.

What does the world need from the versions of you who are calm, clear,
energized, creative, and open?

What if those versions are already in the room?

What if they've been here all along—waiting for you to believe in them?

So if you hear a whisper of something in your soul today… don't ignore it.

Don't wait for certainty or perfection or applause.

Just listen.

And then… gently, bravely, begin.

Because the version of us who finishes things?
They're not a fantasy.
They're real.
They're ready.
And the world needs us—now.

# PART II: CHAPTER 6

# It's All Been Said—But Not by You

*When Your Words Might Be the Real Truth They Hear*

A longtime friend told me she'd been reading some of my earlier writing.
And then she said something that caught me completely off guard:

"Some of this is very basic. Most healers already know this."

Now, I'd love to tell you I smiled and said, "Thank you,"
and moved on with my day.
But that's not what happened.

What happened was... I got upset.
Not just offended, but personally rattled.
Because this wasn't just a comment about something I'd written.
It poked a tender spot—a familiar one.

I started to spiral:

"Maybe she's right. Maybe this isn't deep enough.
Maybe this work isn't needed.
Maybe I shouldn't be doing this at all."

And underneath all of that, something deeper stirred.
Because in that moment, I wasn't just doubting what I had done.

I was doubting what I had expressed.
And whether I even had the right to say it.

And that right there is the moment this chapter was born.

Because I could have easily decided to stop writing altogether.
Or worse, rewrite what I had written to please someone else, to second-guess
what I knew was true for me.

But instead, I paused.
And I asked myself something different.

## THE QUESTION THAT BROUGHT ME BACK
That spiral of doubt led me back to a question I've come to know well.

Not: "Is this good enough?"
"Will people approve?"

But simply: **"What does the world need me to say right now?"**

Not what it needs from someone else.
Not what sounds impressive.
But what's mine to say.

And the answer that came wasn't groundbreaking.
It wasn't even new.

But it was real.
It was honest.
And it had been waiting.

## THE WORDS THAT WAIT IN US
And I realized—this isn't just about me.
This is about all of us.

Because I think every single one of us has had a moment
where we felt something rise in us—
a truth, a message, a knowing—
and we didn't say it.

We hesitated.
We doubted.
We told ourselves someone else could say it better.
Or it's been said before.
Or we're not ready.

And so the moment passed.
The words stayed locked inside.

And I've done that more times than I can count.

## THE COST OF SILENCE

And when I really look at why, it's not because the words weren't ready.
It's because I didn't want to be misunderstood.
Or dismissed.
Or told it wasn't good enough.

But I've learned something:

It's not humility when I hold back what I'm called to say.
It's fear.
And when I let fear stop me, I'm not protecting anyone—
I'm turning away from myself.

Because I did feel something worth saying.
And that feeling came from somewhere deeper than ego.

## WHAT WE MISS WHEN WE DON'T SAY IT

And what about the people who never do speak?

The ones who carry their truth quietly for years.
The people who die with their story still inside them.
The loved ones who kept something locked inside, and we always wondered what it was.
The version of you that wanted to speak—but didn't.

That's not just a personal loss.
That's a collective one.
Because every voice that stays silent…
is a note missing from the song.

The world doesn't just need more content.
It needs your expression.
Your honesty.
Your language, your tone, your timing.

Because the thing that's been said a hundred times?
Might finally land when it comes through you.

## ALL THE WAYS WE SAY IT
And when I talk about what we almost didn't say—
I don't just mean speaking out loud.

I mean that thing you were going to write.
The letter you thought about sending.
The social media post you drafted and deleted.
The idea you had for a blog, a book, a journal entry.

I mean the poem you started and never finished.
The lyrics that came to you on a walk but never made it to paper.
The melody that lived in your body but never left your lips.

The moment you wanted to tell someone the truth—
"I love you."
"I'm scared."
"I need help."
"I'm proud of you."
Or even just, "This is who I really am."

It's all communication.
It's all sacred.
And it all counts.

Because what the world needs from you isn't just action.
It needs honest expression.
In words, in music, in movement, in whatever form it takes.

It's your truth, expressed in the way only you can.
Maybe there's something inside you right now—
not huge or perfect or finished—
but real.
And rising.

A truth that's been waiting.
A message with your name on it.
The one you almost didn't say.

Say it anyway.

Say it gently.
Say it honestly.
Say it imperfectly.

But please… don't let it stay locked inside.

Because someone, somewhere, is waiting to hear it—
**from you.**

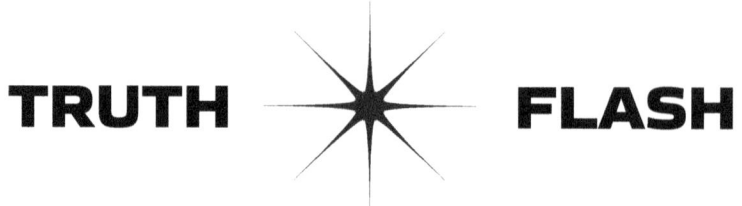

# TRUTH ✴ FLASH

## *THE CREATOR'S CONUNDRUM*

**"IT'S ALREADY BECOME SOMETHING ELSE."**

You return to something you once loved—
a project, a paragraph, a piece of music—
and feel... distant.

Not because it's wrong.
Not because it's bad.
But because *you've changed*.

You're not the same person who made it.

The passion you once had for it?
Moved.
Not from fear. Not from procrastination.
It just... shifted.

And now, your hands finally have the time
to finish what your heart once burned to make—
but the burn is gone.
The fire moved somewhere else.

So what do you do?

Do you shape it again?
Polish it?
Set it free?

Or was it never meant to be published—
just lived?

Was it a cocoon?
A sacred space for the wings you're now using to fly?

This is the artist's tension.
The creator's quiet ache.

Sometimes, the truest thing you can do
is release it—exactly as it is.
To bless the version of you who made it
without dragging it into who you are now.

Other times, the truest thing
is to let it go completely—
and follow the thread that's pulling you now.

Both choices are holy.
Both are brave.
And only *you* will know which one is yours.

# Abraham-Hicks Ruined Complaining for Me Forever

### WHY ALIGNMENT ISN'T OPTIONAL ANYMORE (AND NEITHER IS JOY)

Before I discovered Abraham-Hicks, I thought I was just being honest. Just processing. Just "keeping it real." Just venting with nuance and flair.

Abraham says, "Complaining is arguing for your limitations. And when you do that, we have to agree with you. And that doesn't help."

Oof. Right?

### THE UNIVERSE DOESN'T RESPOND TO WHAT YOU WANT— IT RESPONDS TO WHAT YOU PRACTICE

I used to think you could talk about how bad things were and still attract something better.

But Abraham teaches something wild: You can't talk about what's wrong and activate what's right at the same time.

### ENERGY DOESN'T MULTITASK.

Every time you describe the problem, especially in detail, you light it up again. You lay more track for that same train to keep showing up.

That's not negativity. That's just frequency management.

## THE GREATEST HITS OF ABRAHAM (A QUICK TOUR)

To understand this chapter—and your own ability to manifest anything—here's a quick tour of Abraham-Hicks fundamentals:

### THE VORTEX

The energetic holding zone for everything you've ever wanted. It exists. It's real. You just have to align with it emotionally and vibrationally to let it in.

### THE GRID

The vibrational framework building beneath the surface of your reality. When you feel good, the grid fills in with experiences, people, and things that match that frequency.

### THE EMOTIONAL GUIDANCE SYSTEM

Your feelings are feedback. Not flaws. Not facts. Just indicators of how close you are to alignment with your desires.

### RESISTANCE AND ALLOWING

Resistance = thoughts that contradict your desire. Allowing = relaxing into thoughts that feel better.

"Stop efforting. Start allowing."

## HOW COMPLAINING GOT ME KICKED OUT OF MY OWN ALIGNMENT

Once I started learning from Abraham, I began noticing how often people around me would say things like:

"It's just been one thing after another."
"No one wants to work anymore."
"I never get a break."
"I just need the Universe to throw me a bone."
They weren't expressing clarity. They were rehearsing stuckness.

And those phrases? They weren't helping anyone shift. They were just keeping the same vibration on repeat.

## REALIGNMENT IN REAL TIME

So what do you say instead?

Here are a few common complaints—and their vibrational upgrades:

COMPLAINT: "Nothing's working."
UPGRADE: "Something is always working, even if I can't see it yet."

COMPLAINT: "I'm so tired of this."
UPGRADE: "This is temporary. I'm moving through it."

COMPLAINT: "People keep letting me down."
UPGRADE: "I'm learning to trust my instincts and set better boundaries."

COMPLAINT: "I'm overwhelmed."
UPGRADE: "I'm giving myself permission to slow down and breathe."

And sometimes? You don't say anything. You take a walk. You take a breath. You take a nap.

Because rest is alignment, too.

## GENERAL FIRST. SPECIFIC LATER.

One of the best Abraham tools?

Go general before you go specific.

When you're in a low mood, don't try to write your next great affirmation. Just say something like:

"Things are always working out for me." "This is temporary."
"I've felt like this before and come out stronger."

## JOY IS NOT A LUXURY. IT'S THE PORTAL.

There's a reason Abraham always returns to one word: joy.

Because when you're in joy—or even close to it—you're in alignment. You're in receiving mode. You're magnetic. Clear. Lit up.

Joy isn't the reward. It's the path.

"You get everything you want when you're having fun on the way there."

So if you're not having fun, pause. Pivot. Pet the dog. Hug the kitty. Dance to a song. Reach for anything that lifts you one emotional inch.

## ALIGNMENT ISN'T PERFECTION. IT'S REPETITION.

You won't get this right every time.

But with practice, you'll catch yourself earlier. You'll stop mid-complaint. You'll reframe more naturally. You'll let yourself off the hook faster.

And that's when the Vortex starts delivering.

## FINAL THOUGHT:

"The Universe isn't listening to your words. It's listening to your vibration."

And the great news? Your vibration is something you can shift—
breath by breath, thought by thought, laugh by laugh.

This chapter isn't about censoring yourself. It's about empowering yourself.

Because you don't need to explain what's wrong anymore.
You came here to live what's right.

And it all starts the moment you stop telling the story you don't want—
and start feeling your way into the one you do.

# TRUTH  FLASH

## *The Drip*
## *When Your Alignment Starts to Show*

AUTHOR'S NOTE:
*If you don't know what The Drip is, don't worry—*
*it doesn't require ointment.*

In pop culture, having "drip" means you've got style,
swagger, that unmissable something.
You're radiating. Flowing. Drenched in your own vibe.

So let's talk about what happens when your alignment starts to show—
in ways the world can't ignore.

**You don't have to shout it.**
**You don't even have to try.**

When you're aligned...
You drip.

Not with sweat from the hustle.
Not with stress from the striving.

You drip with presence.
With power.
With peace that doesn't need to be explained.

It's in the way you stand.
The way you listen.
The way your smile says, "I already got the download."

Your drip is divine.
A holy swagger.
Vortex chic.

People feel it when you walk in the room.
Not because you said something wise—
but because your Being said it for you.

You're not faking the drip.
You are it.

Every step. Every look. Every choice.
An echo of the you who already knows.

So go ahead.
Walk like heaven's got your back.
Smile like the Grid's already working.

And let the world catch a little of your sacred spill.

Because when you're truly in the Vortex?

You don't just glow.
You drip.

# PART II: CHAPTER 8

# Deepak Said: "I'm Not My Emotions." And Honestly? Same.

*What to Do With All These Feelings You're Not Supposed to Have*

**INTRO NOTE:** If you're wondering about the word *"same"* in the title—it's a nod to modern slang and online culture. "Same" is the kind of thing people say when something hits a little too close to home. Not with a big emotional speech, just a dry little "yep." So when Deepak said, *"I am not my emotions,"* I didn't argue. I just nodded and said it too: *Same.*

There are some phrases so serene and calmly radical they feel like whispered instructions from another realm. Deepak Chopra is full of them.

"I am not my emotions. I am not my thoughts. I am awareness."

Sounds peaceful, right?

Unless, of course, you're in the middle of a shame spiral or crying in your car. Then it feels like one of those spiritual bumper stickers you want to peel off with your fingernails.

But still... something in you knows he's right.

Because you are the one noticing the emotion.
You are the one watching the thought.

And if you can notice it, then maybe you aren't entirely inside it—
or it isn't entirely inside you.
Maybe you're bigger than it.
Maybe you're the sky, not the storm.

This chapter is where Deepak joins the conversation. One of his core teachings:

You are not the content of your awareness. You are the awareness itself.

It sounds abstract. But it changes everything.

## SO WHAT DOES THAT ACTUALLY MEAN?

If you are not your thoughts or emotions... then who are you?

Deepak would say you're the one who's aware. The witness.
The still point behind the noise.

This isn't about not feeling. It's about learning to watch the feeling
rather than become it.

Imagine this: You feel anxious.
You say to yourself, "I notice I'm feeling anxious."

Suddenly, there's a gap—a breath—between you and the anxiety.

In that space, you can choose.
To breathe. To sit. To ask what's true. To stay instead of run.
That space is awareness. That space is your power.

## THE PRACTICE OF BECOMING THE OBSERVER

Here's how Deepak teaches us to live from awareness:

1.  **Notice** what you're feeling—without judgment.
2.  **Name** it gently. ("Sadness is here." "Frustration is present.")
3.  **Breathe** into the moment, not away from it.
4.  **Remember** you are not the storm or these clouds of emotions. You are
    the sky they move through.

The miracle isn't that the feeling disappears.
The miracle is that you remember who you are while it moves.

## TRY THIS: THE 90-SECOND RESET

Close your eyes.

Take a slow breath.

Say quietly, "I am the one watching this."

Let the feeling rise.

Stay.

Watch.

Wait for the feeling to soften, even a little.

Say, "This, too, is passing through."

Repeat the breath.

Open your eyes.

"You are not here to fight the storm.
You are here to remember that you are the sky."

## NOT BYPASSING. NOT SUPPRESSING. JUST BEING.

You can still feel deeply. You can still cry and rage and grieve and giggle.
You're just not confusing those temporary visitors with your permanent self.

This isn't spiritual detachment.
It's spiritual homecoming.

Because the truth is:

Emotions are weather.
Thoughts are waves.
And you? You are the ocean.

## PART II: CHAPTER 9

# The One-Two Punch:
# When Practice Becomes Power

I didn't want to be spiritual. I wanted to be right.
That's how the argument started.

It wasn't loud. But the energy between us had turned sharp—quiet and sharp, which is often worse. I said something that sounded reasonable in my head, and it landed wrong. The other person responded with something equally reasonable. And suddenly we were both standing there, armed with our reasons, silently daring the other to let theirs go first.

And I felt it—that flush of heat in my chest, the tightness in my stomach, the story forming in my head about what they always do, what I never get, and why I was clearly the one who should be hurt here.

I almost stayed there.
I almost chose the version of me who gets righteous. Who shuts down and lets it simmer. I've been that version before. I know the script.

But this time… I paused.
Not because I'm better. Not because I'm evolved.
But because I remembered something I'd practiced enough to feel it rise on its own.

## THE FIRST PUNCH IS AWARENESS.

That's Deepak's territory.

I remembered: I am not this story. I am the awareness of the story.

So I stepped back—not physically, but internally.
I became the sky.
And I watched the emotions—frustration, hurt, heat—float through me like clouds. I didn't chase them. I didn't name them. I just noticed them.

They weren't me.
They were just weather.

And in that moment, something opened.
Not because I figured it out. But because I remembered who I was: Not the cloud. The sky.

That was the shift. That was the breath.

## THE SECOND PUNCH IS EMOTIONAL.

That's Abraham's domain.

Once I wasn't tangled in the story, I could feel my way forward with clean hands.

I had dropped the resistance. Now I could reach for relief.

So I asked:

- What would peace feel like right now?
- What if this moment wasn't about winning?
- What would the Vortex version of me do?

And I didn't have to fake the answers. They showed up on their own:

- I've misunderstood people before.
- They care about me.
- This doesn't have to be anything more than what it is.

And then… click.
The vibration rose.
The version of me I actually wanted to be came back online.

Not through force.
Through release.

And something else happened, too.
The other person softened.
Not because I won the moment. Not because I said the right thing.
But because the energy I was holding stopped fighting. And it made room for
both of us to feel safe again.

## THAT'S THE ONE-TWO PUNCH.
First: Remember who you are.
Then: Choose how you want to feel.

Let Deepak clear the fog.
Let Abraham light the way.

Sometimes I forget both steps. Sometimes I circle back later. But when I catch
it—when I remember I'm not the cloud, and then climb the ladder back to joy—

It's not just peace.
It's power.
It's the moment the message becomes real in me.

And it works.
Even when I don't want to be spiritual.
Even when I want to be right.

# Complaining and What the World Doesn't Need to Hear From Us Now

*A Guide to Not Wasting Your Breath*

We all do it. The little sigh.
The eye-roll.
The extra detail added to the story to make someone really get how bad it was.
The dig disguised as a joke.
The "just saying" that's really just complaining.

And sometimes we tell ourselves it's harmless.

But the truth is—every time we say something that drops our energy,
we're lowering the drawbridge to resistance.
And that beautiful frequency we've been working so hard to hold?

Gone.
Flattened.
Traded for a temporary hit of shared frustration.

## LET'S BE HONEST: NOT EVERYTHING NEEDS TO BE SAID OUT LOUD

Especially not the low-vibe stuff. That comment about how lazy people are?
That sigh about how expensive everything is?
That observation about how the world's going to hell?

None of it helps.
Not you.
Not them.
Not your Vortex.

"The Universe is always listening. But more importantly, *you're* always listening. Every sentence you speak is either reinforcing alignment—or arguing against it."

## THE SILENT KILLER OF ALIGNMENT: HABITUAL COMPLAINT

Every time a little moan slips out—about the body, the partner, the work, the world—it doesn't just vent pressure.

It drags the signal downward.

And the Vortex?
The Vortex is calibrated to your highest joy, your most stable ease, your lightest laughter.

When we drop into criticism, sarcasm, chronic worry, or any of the "I'm just being real" vibes—we walk ourselves right out of receiving mode.

**"There's no such thing as a neutral complaint.
Every negative statement is a vote for misalignment."**

## TRY THE BREATH TEST

Before you speak, try this fast internal check:

- Take a breath.
- Ask: Will this raise the vibe or lower it?
- Ask again: Is this adding peace, clarity, possibility—or just noise?
- Decide: Speak it if it helps the energy move. Zip it if it's just another episode in the story rerun.

## A (PARTIALLY SARCASTIC) LIST OF THINGS THE WORLD DOESN'T NEED TO HEAR RIGHT NOW

"It's just hard for people like me."
"There's never enough time."
"No one ever listens."
"Nothing ever works out the way I hope."
"It's always something."
"I'm just so tired of being the one who has to…"
"Why does this always happen to me?"
"Must be nice to have that kind of money."
"People are so [insert judgment here]."

Each of these might feel like sharing.
But energetically? They're like spreading mud on a clean window.

## WHAT TO SAY INSTEAD

Let your voice become a tuning fork for your desires. Not fake, not forced.
But upgraded.

Try:

- "This is shifting."
- "Something good is unfolding here."
- "Even though I don't get it yet, I trust it's working in my favor."
- "I'm feeling something new come in."
- "The energy's starting to move."

These are phrases the Universe leans toward.
These are the permission slips your Vortex has been waiting for.

## WHY THIS MATTERS SO MUCH (ESPECIALLY NOW)

We're not just here to feel a little better.
We're here to become the miracle.
To live from the frequency of what we want—so the world can see what alignment looks like.

But every low-vibe throwaway comment pulls the plug a little.

It's not about being perfect.
It's about caring enough to pause.

Because your words aren't just sound. They're energy placement devices.

So when you choose not to complain, not to judge, not to snark or moan or explain why it's so hard? You're not suppressing.
You're aligning.

"Every time you don't say the thing that would have lowered your vibe, you just got closer to everything you want."

## FINAL WORD

You don't have to be a guru.
You don't have to float through life with white robes and a prayer voice.

But if you want to live a miraculous life—
If you want to feel free, creative, joyful, lit up—
Then what you say has to match what you're calling in.

Speak like the miracle is already happening.
And if it doesn't lift the room, open the door, light the path, or honor your becoming—
let it die on your tongue.

Your next miracle might depend on it.

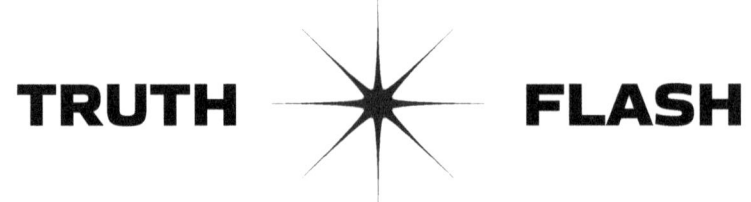

# TRUTH ✳ FLASH

## *The Original Self Before the Scars*

Some people have lives that look complete.
Beautiful marriages.
Work that matters.
Laughter at the dinner table.
Photos full of smiles.

And still—
something flickers at the edge of it all.

It's not exactly pain.
Not exactly trauma.
It's a presence.
The one you haven't fully let in.

The one who danced before anyone told you how.
Who didn't wait to be good at something before loving it.
Who didn't ask for permission before stepping into the light.

We talk about healing the inner child like she's broken.
But what if she's not?
What if she's the most brilliant part of you?

What if the version of you that gets everything done,
is missing the one who used to do things for no reason at all?

That's the Original Self.
She's not your past.
She's not your pain.
She's the part of you that still knows how to be fully alive—
before the filters, the roles, the applause.

You don't have to undo the life you've built.
You just have to let her in.

Not to take over—
but to remind you what it feels like to laugh without editing,
to create without bracing for feedback,
to trust joy before it proves itself.

She's not gone.
She didn't disappear under your responsibilities.
She just got quiet.

She's been watching you survive.
Watching you lead.

Watching you love others through storms.
And she's proud of you.

But now—she wants in.

Not to fix you.
To play with you.
To surprise you.
To hand you back your ease.

She came to say the one thing no one else can:

"You were always the miracle."

Not because you earned it.
But because you carried something sacred the whole way—
even when you forgot it was there.

She was the spark in the tunnel.
The softness behind your strength.
The reason the message still got through.

And maybe that's what made the miracle possible:
You didn't lose her.
You just forgot she was the key.

Now she's knocking.
Not demanding—
Just asking:
"Can I come with you now?"

That's what changes everything.

When your current self—structured, successful, maybe cautious—
has finally softened enough to welcome back the spontaneous, joyful,
vulnerable part of you.

When the miracle you've been chasing
starts to sound like your own laughter.
When the one you once left behind
becomes the one who walks you home.

# PART II: CHAPTER 11

# Maybe It Wasn't About You

*When You're the Blessing in Someone Else's Story*

Sometimes the moment isn't about you.
You think you're just going somewhere.
You think you're the audience:
But you're the message.
You're the answer to someone else's question.
You're the reminder they asked the Universe to send.

I've had so many moments in my life when it seemed like coincidence. But after it happened again and again, I realized: some moments aren't about us—they're for the other person in the story.

Like when we went to France and got lost two times in as many days. People showed up, seemingly out of nowhere, to help us. But I believe those moments weren't just for us—they were for the people who helped.

Like the young Algerian man in Marseille who guided us to a hotel when the GPS failed. Or the Portuguese man who spent an hour walking the city and riding the trolley with us until we found the perfect place to stay.

Maybe we were just bit players in *their* story—the reason they got to feel helpful, kind, and needed. The moment they went home and told their wives, "I helped a couple of nice Americans today."

That's what it means to be a messenger.
Not because you know something, but because you showed up.
Because you said yes to aligning first—and trusting what unfolds next.

And when you live like that—when you walk into rooms remembering that your
presence might be the very thing someone else prayed for—you start to feel it:
the miracle moving through you.

That's when grace shows up unannounced.
When glory hums quietly in the background.
When providence reintroduces you to who you really are.

## LIVING THE WORDS

Grace. Glory. Providence.
Each one beautiful on its own—but when you begin to experience yourself as the
messenger, you begin to witness the very moments those words were made for.

That ease that shouldn't have come?
Grace.
That shimmer in the room after your kindness landed?
Glory.
That timing you couldn't have orchestrated?
Providence.

Because when you live in alignment,
you don't just believe in miracles—
you start to speak them.
You start to become them.

You're not just here to get by.
You're here to become the one the world—and you—have been waiting for.

The one who says yes when it would be easier to walk past.
The one who holds a gaze long enough for someone else to feel seen.
The one who shows up, again and again, not to be noticed—
but to deliver what only you can bring.

You are the quiet answer to someone's silent prayer.
Their miracle disguised as the ordinary.

# PART II: CHAPTER 12

# The Clean Energy of Letting Go

*(The Step You Can't Skip on the Way to Becoming the Miracle)*

There's a point in almost every deep transformation where everything gets quiet.
Not clear. Not euphoric.
Just… still.

You've done the work.
You've faced the scar.
You've invited the original self—the little one who left too early—back home.
You've climbed the emotional altimeter and steadied your breath.
You're aligned.

And yet—nothing's moving.
Nothing's shifting.
The room feels the same.

This is where people lose their way.
Not because they weren't ready.
But because they thought *readiness was enough.*

They thought alignment meant results.
That once you came home to yourself, the miracle would come rushing in.

Here's what no one tells you:

**Alignment isn't the finish line. It's the threshold.**
And just beyond it… is the step almost everyone skips:

**Detachment.**

## WHAT DETACHMENT ACTUALLY IS
Detachment is not apathy.
It's not disengagement.
It's not pretending not to care.

It's the moment you stop grasping.
It's the release of energetic need.
It's saying, "I've shown up. I've done the work.
And now, I don't need this moment to prove anything."

It's not a performance.
It's not a surrender to failure.
It's a surrender **to freedom.**

## WHERE THE WISDOM COMES FROM
This step isn't new.

In the spiritual traditions of India, it's been revered for thousands of years.

In **Hinduism**, it's called *vairāgya (vy-RAHG-yuh)*—a sacred dispassion.
In the Bhagavad Gita, Krishna tells Arjuna:

*"You have the right to your actions, but not to the fruits of your actions."*

Take action. Stay aligned.
But let go of the outcome.

In **Buddhism**, it's *upekkhā (oo-PEK-kah)*—equanimity.
You don't lose your heart. You just stop clinging to how things unfold.

In **Jainism**, it's *aparigraha (uh-PUH-rih-grah-huh)*—non-possessiveness.
You stop trying to own what's not yours to hold.
Even your hopes.

These traditions didn't teach detachment to avoid life.
They taught it to **set the soul free**.

## WHY YOU NEED THIS STEP

Because even when you're aligned… your energy can still be *gripping*.
Wanting, proving, checking, hoping.

Even after you've welcomed your original self back into your heart…
You might be trying to perform the miracle, just to make sure it was all worth it.

But miracles don't arrive on command.
They don't respond to panic, or performance, or desperation dressed up as positivity.

They respond to **clean energy.**

**When you stop needing to create the outcome, your energy gets clean.
And from that place… the world bends in your direction.**

Not because you forced it.
But because you *stopped distorting it.*

That's detachment.

The moment you open your hands—
and the universe finally has somewhere to put the gift.

## HOW YOU KNOW YOU'RE THERE

You don't always *feel* the miracle land.
But here's what you do feel:

- Your chest loosens.
- You stop trying to impress the room.
- You sleep better.
- You say, "Whatever happens, I'm okay."
- And this time… you mean it.

You don't walk in to shift the room.

You walk in **already shifted.**

And the miracle?
It doesn't need to announce itself.

It just finds you.
Because you're not blocking it anymore.

So many of us thought the miracle would come after the work.
After the forgiveness.
After the healing.
After the breakthrough.

But the miracle was never something you summoned.
It's something that slips in when you stop chasing it.

Not because you stopped wanting it.
But because you stopped *needing* it to happen a certain way.

And from that place of clean energy…
From that place of sacred detachment…

You're ready.

**The miracle is next.**
And this time,
you won't miss it.

# PART II: CHAPTER 13

## The One Who Became the Miracle

It doesn't happen with fanfare.
You don't wake up glowing.
There's no halo. No applause.
You just notice…
Life starts answering differently.

You think something—and it shows up.
You whisper a hope—and someone else names it out loud.
You wonder if you're on the right path—
and a feather drops in front of you,
or a stranger says exactly what you needed to hear.

It's not magic.
It's alignment.
It's awareness.
It's becoming the version of you that life has been trying to
partner with all along.

Because when you really align—not just spiritually, but emotionally,
energetically, practically—
you don't just feel better.
You become a tuning fork for the miraculous.

You show up differently now—calmer, clearer—and people feel it.
Doors open without you knocking.
You get seated next to the right person, again and again.

You say yes to the invitation you almost declined—
and it turns into the connection you didn't know you needed.

It starts to feel like grace got your address.
Like timing started obeying your trust.
Like your life is now complicit with goodness.

Coincidences pile up too perfectly to explain.
Messages come in from places you can't plan.
And something quiet inside you says,
"This is what it feels like when God gets bolder in your life."

Not because God changed.
But because you did.

You stopped arguing with the spark.
You stopped delaying joy.
You stopped believing you needed to be more healed,
more polished,
more ready.

You just... aligned.
And everything changed.

This is what it means to become the miracle.
Not to be worshipped.
Not to be perfect.
But to be the living proof that:

Love is real.
Timing is sacred.
Healing is possible.
Presence is enough.

You've spent years hoping for miracles.
And maybe you received a few.
But this is different.

This is the moment you realize:
You don't just wait for them anymore.
You are one.

And maybe this book, this journey, this breath you're taking right now...
is the opening of something bigger than you knew to expect.

You are no longer the one chasing light.
You are the one carrying it.

So keep going.
Keep aligning.
Keep whispering yes.

The world is already shifting in your direction.
Because the miracle didn't *come* to you.

**Now, the miracle, *is* you.**

# GLOSSARY OF BECOMING

*Key Terms and Truth Flashes from the Miracle*

### ABRAHAM-HICKS
The collective consciousness channeled by Esther Hicks, whose teachings center around the Law of Attraction. Concepts like the Vortex, the Grid, and emotional alignment originate from this source.

### ALIGNMENT
A state where your thoughts, emotions, and energy are congruent with your true self. In alignment, you become a match to what's in your Vortex.

### APARIGRAHA (AH-PAH-REE-GRAH-HAH)
From Sanskrit, meaning "non-grasping" or "non-possessiveness." A foundational yogic principle that invites you to release control, comparison, and the compulsion to hold tightly. *Aparigraha* is what makes room for overflow.

### ALLOWING
The emotional state that lets your desires flow to you. It's the practice of softening resistance and trusting the process.

### AWARENESS
The pure, observing presence beneath all thought. As Deepak Chopra teaches, it's not your emotions or thoughts—but the container in which they happen.

### BECOMING
The process of stepping into the next version of yourself. It is both active and surrendered—a co-creation with Source.

### CONTRAST
Experiences that clarify your desires by showing you what you don't want. Abraham-Hicks describes it as essential to expansion.

## CREATOR'S CONUNDRUM *(Truth Flash)*

The dilemma of the artist who has outgrown the very work they once burned to create.

## DETACHMENT

The Step You Can't Skip

Not apathy. Not giving up. Detachment is the energetic release of needing the outcome. It's the quiet trust that what's meant for you won't miss you— and that your readiness doesn't require proof. A deep spiritual practice in many traditions, detachment clears the final bit of static between you and the miracle.

## THE DRIP (TRUTH FLASH)

When your alignment becomes visible—through energy, ease, or presence. True drip doesn't strive, it flows.

## EMOTIONAL GUIDANCE SYSTEM

Your emotions are not mistakes but messages. They tell you how close or far you are from alignment with Source.

## ENVY: THE ECHO OF A LIFE YOU HAVEN'T CHOSEN YET *(Truth Flash)*

Envy is not about what others have—it's a signal toward something in you that still longs to be lived.

## INNER BEING

The higher, wiser part of you that sees from a broader perspective and always remains in the Vortex.

## LET THEM LOVE YOU OUT LOUD *(Truth Flash)*

Receiving love is just as spiritual as giving it. Letting others bless you honors the Universe speaking through them.

## MIRACLE

Not something you wait for, but something you become. A miracle is alignment in action—a blessing you become for others.

## NONLOCAL SELF

A Deepak Chopra term referring to the self beyond biography or boundaries. This version of you already exists in the field of all possibilities.

## ORIGINAL SELF *(Truth Flash)*

Before the pain, before the applause—there's a version of you who was fully alive. She's not gone. She's just waiting for your invitation.

## PARALLEL LIVES

The vibrational versions of you that still exist and can be stepped into through alignment. These aren't lost—just waiting.

## PRESENCE

Showing up fully, without trying to change, fix, or flee the moment. Presence is the gateway to grace.

## RESISTANCE

Thoughts or emotions that contradict your desire. It's the vibration of "no" to your own asking—and the root of most struggle.

## SACRED COW

A belief or habit you protect—even when it no longer serves you. Sacred cows often block growth because we're afraid to question them.

## SOURCE

The divine intelligence or spiritual current of life. Source is always calling you forward—toward more joy, love, and freedom.

## THE DRESSING ROOM

A metaphor for your inner space of transformation and preparation. Not everyone deserves access while you're still becoming.

## THE EMPTY CUP

A symbol of readiness. Emptiness isn't failure—it means you've made space for what's next.

## THE GRID
Abraham-Hicks' term for the energetic framework that precedes manifestation. Build the emotional grid, and the details fill in.

## THE SCAR
The visible or invisible evidence of your journey. Loving the scar means honoring your wholeness—including what hurt.

## THE SEASON
Not everything is meant to last forever. Some things—like the birds and flowers—are sacred because they were brief.

## THE TUNNEL
The place of challenge, confusion, and growth. The tunnel becomes a temple when you don't run from the darkness.

## THE VORTEX
A key Abraham-Hicks concept: the vibrational space where all your desires exist. You align with the Vortex through joy.

## THE VOICE WITHIN (Truth Theme)
Encouragement to speak, act, and walk from the deeper truth already alive in you.

## UPEKKHĀ (OO-PEK-KHA)
A Pali word translated as "equanimity." This is not detachment in the cold sense, but the spacious, calm awareness that allows all experiences to rise and fall without resistance. A quality of inner stillness that helps you stay aligned through both joy and loss.

## VAIRĀGYA (VY-RAHG-YAH)
A Sanskrit word meaning "dispassion" or "freedom from attachment." In yogic philosophy, vairāgya refers to the quiet strength of letting go—not to abandon desire, but to stop clinging to it. Vairāgya opens space for grace to move.

## VIBRATION
Your dominant frequency—based on your thoughts and feelings—that determines what you attract.

# AUTHOR'S NOTE:
# HOW THE BOOK FOUND ME

This was always going to be a book.
Just not like this.

It started as a kind of "Abraham for Dummies"—a simplified translation of the principles I'd been practicing, whispering to friends, scribbling into notebooks. But somewhere along the way, something else took over. Symbols began to appear. Voices came through. Not spooky, not theatrical—just… present. Persistent. Loving. Clear. A little boy's voice in my head. A metaphor in a dream. A sentence that felt too good to be mine. I have theories—of course I do!—about who some of the voices were. People I've loved. Spirits I've felt. Maybe even a few familiar souls reaching through the veil—

So I followed the trail. And what started as a translation became a transmission. A book not just about alignment, but about becoming.
Not just about the Vortex, but about being the kind of person the world can't help but be changed by.

That's what happened here. The book wrote me as much as I wrote it.

And I didn't do it alone.

To Lorraine—Rain—my partner in all things: business, life, and magic. One of my most memorable moments was when my son Ross's friend Tidus, asked us how we got together. We told him we'd had a couple businesses together first, and then fell in love. He blinked and said, "Ohhh, so you got the bag first!" Still one of my favorite lines. It's funny because it's true: we made things together—ideas, impact, income—and then we built a life. A partnership rooted in love, laughter, and always trying to be the kind of people we hoped others could count on. I was welcomed into her family with full arms and open hearts, and through the eyes of Ross—*my son, who became our son*—I got to see the kind of mother, leader, and light she is. He called her Rain when he was little, and the name stuck. It suits her.

To my parents and my brother: thank you for the love and the sparks. For the creativity, the encouragement, the music, the words, the ideas. For always filling the air with something to dream into. My brother was my earliest muse, the one who made imagination feel like a calling. And my parents filled our world with love and originality—and just enough wildness and freedom to make anything feel possible.

To Ross—your talent is pure joy. Your commitment to what you love, even when the odds say otherwise, inspires me daily. You remind me to keep going, to keep dreaming, and to trust the inner knowing that brought you—and me—this far.

To Gus, my cat of 19 years: thank you for sitting in silence when I needed it, meowing when I didn't know I needed it, and just being that quiet, furry guardian through life's in-betweens. There are love stories that don't need words, and we had one.

To John Lonergan, head of the Department of Design at Southern Illinois University, who taught me that being a creative wasn't just about ideas—it was about impact. About showing up in the world and offering something real. He gave me a handshake that changed my life—firm, certain, generous. I've never shaken a hand since without thinking of that grip. It became part of me.

To Maria Galleta, who showed me what it looks like when love puts on walking shoes. You are my own Mother Theresa. You reminded me that service isn't a duty—it's an overflow of compassion. My work with immigrants and the homeless was made sacred by people like you.

To our dear friend Chrissy, who designed the book in its whole divine essence!

To God. To the Divine Spark. To the Whisper that never stopped whispering. You keep showing up. Thank You.

This book didn't come from me. It came *through* me. But it came through a life shaped by all of you. And now, I offer it forward.

May it be light in the places you forgot you could still glow.
May it meet you in the moment you need it most.
And may it remind you that what the world needs next…
might be waiting to come through *you.*

With love,
Doug

# ABOUT THE AUTHOR

**DOUG COOPER** is a spiritual teacher, writer, and retired entrepreneur who believes the real miracle isn't something you find—it's something you become.

After years in business and nonprofit leadership, Doug turned his focus to what he calls "the work beneath the work"—helping people remember who they really are and why the world needs them now. He has taught English to immigrants, built innovative programs for the homeless, and guided people back to joy through quiet moments of deep listening.

Doug blends spiritual insight with everyday wisdom, drawing from Abraham-Hicks, Deepak Chopra, and decades of lived experience. He speaks, writes, and creates from San Diego, California—always guided by one recurring question:

*What does the world need from us now?*

———

www.dougcooper.com